The
WORLD
CUP

Published by Creative Education, Inc.
123 South Broad Street, Mankato, MN 56001

Designed by Rita Marshall with the help of Thomas Lawton
Cover illustration by Rob Day, Lance Hidy Associates

Photography by Allsport, Bob Thomas,
Focus on Sports, Globe Photos, Photri,
Wide World Photos

Printed in the United States

Library of Congress Cataloging-in-Publication Data

Goodman, Michael E.
    Soccer's World Cup/by Michael E. Goodman.
    p.   cm.—(Great moments in sports)
    Summary: Surveys the history of soccer and its prestigious World
Cup competition.
    ISBN 0-88682-320-X
    1. World Cup (Soccer)—History—Juvenile literature. [1. World
Cup (Soccer)—History. 2. Soccer—History.] I. Title. II. Series.
GV943.49.G66   1989   89-29999
796.334'66—dc20   CIP
                                                              AC

The WORLD CUP

MICHAEL GOODMAN

CREATIVE EDUCATION INC.

5

More than 110,000 fans watched as the Brazilian soccer player with amazingly powerful legs broke toward the Italian goal. The Brazilian was known only by his nickname, Pelé, but that one name was one of the most famous in all the sports world.

Pelé dribbled the soccer ball past two Italian defenders, then passed it off to the right and headed for a spot directly in front of the goal. His teammate, Rivelino, spotted Pelé near the goal and sent a crossing kick toward him. Pelé stretched his five-and-a-half-foot body as high as it would go and headed the ball past a dazed Italian goaltender and into the net.

It was the first goal in the 1970 World Cup final game and Pelé's last in World Cup competition, and it set off a wild celebration in Mexico City and around the world. The crowd in the stadium rose to cheer the goal and the international hero who had scored it. Huddled around television sets or radios in every continent on the globe, more than a billion other people joined in the applause.

Teams around the globe compete for the World's Cup.

A few minutes later, Italian fans had their own reason to cheer as their favorites evened the score. Despite the celebration, it was early in the game and everyone knew anything could happen. The Italians had an explosive offense and could come back in an instant. A few minutes later it happened. After rushing almost the entire length of the field, an Italian forward drilled a hard shot past the stunned Brazilian netminder. The score was once again deadlocked.

The World Cup is the only sporting event that can cause so much excitement and emotion around the globe. One reason for this is that soccer is the world's most popular sport. It is played both on hard, sun-baked fields in South America and on soft, muddy grounds in Europe. And it is played in any open space in any country by children and adults alike.

Pele scored with a header during the 1970 final.

Every four years, the finest national teams gather for a tournament that is a combination of athletic excellence and national pride. Unlike the World Series, the Super Bowl, or the Stanley Cup, the World Cup is truly a world's championship. While large or populous countries such as Brazil, Italy, West Germany, Argentina, and England have dominated the World Cup finals, smaller countries such as Uruguay, Hungary, Holland, and Czechoslovakia have also made their mark. And one of the greatest upsets in Cup history was achieved by tiny North Korea.

Another famous soccer hero was Gary Lineker from England.

The stars of the World Cup are both national and international heroes. Children around the world have pretended they are Pelé from Brazil, Eusebio from Portugal, Johan Cruyff from Holland, Franz Beckenbauer from West Germany, Paolo Rossi from Italy, or Diego Maradona from Argentina. These children have dreamed of providing soccer fans with the same type of great moments that their heroes have given them.

9

BEGINNINGS

Soccer is not only the most popular game in the world; it is also one of the oldest. More than 2,000 years ago, Chinese soldiers played a game called *tsu chu,* which means "to kick a ball with the feet." Each year on the emperor's birthday, two teams of soldiers would meet on a field and kick a ball toward goalposts thirty feet high. The ancient Greeks also had a game that involved kicking a ball, and Roman soldiers brought a similar game to England when they conquered that island. It was in England that the game called "football" really developed.

In the mid-1800s, young British gentlemen in England's finest schools began playing both football and a game called "rugby football," in which players could pick up the ball in their hands and run with it. That game became the basis for American and Canadian football. In 1863, a group of people who preferred the feet-only ball game instead of rugby formed an organization called the Football Association. The group developed a set of rules for "association football," which they called "soccer" for short.

As British soldiers, sailors, missionaries, miners, and engineers traveled around the world, they played soccer and taught natives of other countries the game. Soon "futbol" was being played throughout Spain, Portugal, and Latin America, and "fussball" was being played in Germany and Eastern Europe. By 1904, an international organization called the Federation Internationale de Football Associations (FIFA) was formed as a governing body for soccer around the world. At its first meeting, FIFA announced that it planned to establish an international championship tournament, to be called the World Cup, but it took twenty-six years before the first tournament was actually staged.

Arguments and politics kept FIFA from establishing its first World Cup tournament until 1930. Every year from 1904 to 1928, the idea of holding an international championship was brought up at FIFA's annual meeting, but no one could decide how and where the tournament would be held. In the end, pride settled the issue. The pride of European soccer players and fans had been hurt when teams from the South American country of Uruguay won the Olympic soccer tournament in 1924 and 1928. According to the rules, only amateurs could play in the Olympics. However, most of the finest European players were professionals. The European countries now pushed for an international competition in which professionals could also take part. So FIFA's president, Jules Rimet of France, began planning the first World Cup to be held in Uruguay in 1930. To honor Rimet for his hard work, the trophy to be presented to the winner was named after him.

Unfortunately, mileage got in the way of the first tournament. Many European nations didn't want to risk sending teams the long distance by boat to South America. Only four teams made the trip across the Atlantic Ocean—Belgium, France, Romania, and Yugoslavia. They were joined by seven South American teams and teams from Mexico and the United States. Yet despite the limited attendance, the first World Cup was an exciting indication of what was to come.

Thousands of fans from around the globe attend World Cup matches.

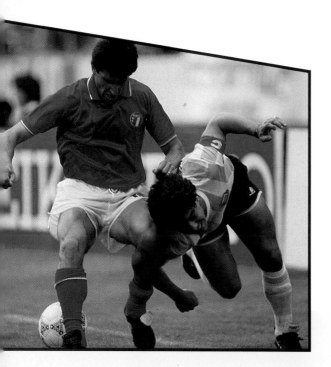

The thirteen squads were organized into four divisions, with the teams in each pool playing each other to decide which one would qualify for the semifinal round. After several closely fought contests, Argentina, the United States, Uruguay, and Yugoslavia emerged as the four division winners.

In the semifinals, Argentina defeated a U.S. team that consisted largely of former Scottish and British players, and the Uruguayans defeated Yugoslavia. That meant that the finalists from the 1928 Olympics, Uruguay and Argentina, would meet again in an all–South America battle.

Both countries took the finals very seriously. Uruguayan fans packed the new stadium in their capital of Montevideo. They were joined by thousands of Argentines who had made the trip to root for their heroes—the great playmaker, Monti, and top scorer, Stabile. Officials expected some fights among fans or players during the game, but there was only one controversy—over which team's ball would be used for the match. In the end, it was decided that the Argentine ball would be used for the first half and the Uruguayan ball for the second. No one knows if the ball made a difference, but the Argentines held a 2–1 lead at halftime, then fell behind in the second half and lost 4–2. For the Uruguayan team and their many fans, it was a great moment they would never forget.

EUROPE VS. SOUTH AMERICA

In the first World Cup, most of the teams had come from South America. In the second tournament, European teams outnumbered the South American teams. Many South American countries didn't send teams to the host country Italy, or sent their less-talented players for fear that European professional teams might steal their best players by offering

In the 1980s, Argentina found another hero in Diego Maradona.

European teams like England and Morocco, shown here in a recent match, dominated the second Cup.

them higher salaries. It had happened before. For example, the Argentine star Monti, who had played so brilliantly for his country in 1930, joined another Argentine great named Orsi in an Italian professional league in 1934. Both men became members of the Italian World Cup team.

The Italian team had other advantages in the tournament as well. During its games, the team received a lot of help from officials, who were afraid to make calls that might anger Italian dictator Benito Mussolini. In one game against Spain, three Spanish players had to be carried off the field with injuries for which Italian players received no penalties. Also, two Spanish goals were disallowed in the game that Italy eventually won 1–0. The Swiss referee in charge of the game was later suspended by his national soccer association for not doing his job properly.

These fans, like those in Rome, were ardent supporters of their team.

With help like this, the Italians reached the finals, where they played one of the most exciting Cup matches ever against Czechoslovakia. The game was scoreless after seventy minutes of the ninety-minute contest. Then a Czech forward took a corner kick, received a return near the net, and shot the ball past the Italian goalie. The fans in Rome went crazy with anger and frustration. Some of the fans even had to be stopped from attacking the Czech players when it seemed they might defeat the hometown favorites for the world title.

15

Then, with eight minutes to go in the match, Orsi, the Argentine now playing for Italy, took a pass from a teammate, faked to his left, then kicked the ball toward the right. The ball curved over the outstretched Czech goalie and into the net. It was an almost impossible shot. The next day, Orsi tried to repeat the shot for reporters but was unsuccessful in twenty tries at an open net.

The tied game went into a thirty-minute overtime period, during which Italy scored the only goal. For the second straight time, the home country had won the World Cup.

THE KING OF SOCCER

Over the next twenty years, soccer and the world struggled. World War II ripped many nations apart, and sports were no longer as important as they had once seemed. But as the world witnessed a great moment with the ending of the war in 1945, the sport of soccer recovered as well. By 1954, a team from Brazil rose to the top of the soccer world as no team had before. Over the next twelve years, the Brazilians would win three of four World Cups and entertain fans with many great moments of soccer action.

What impressed soccer fans most about the Brazilians was not just that they won but how they won. They brought an entirely new style of play to international soccer competition. Most European teams and many Latin American squads utilized a rough, defensive style of soccer, played at a very fast pace up and down the field. There was always lots of physical contact. That's not how the Brazilians played. Their technique involved moving at a slow, steady pace by making lots of short, crisp passes. The Brazilians didn't get as tired as their opponents and escaped injuries by avoiding excess physical contact.

Not every team could follow Brazil's style of play because not many had players like Brazil's two great forwards, known by their nicknames, Vava and Pelé. Both players were fast, accurate, tireless, and unselfish.

Pele (bottom row, third from left) led Brazil to victory in 1958.

Pelé, who was only seventeen years old, was playing in his first international competition in 1958. He was practically unknown before the World Cup, but during that tournament and for the next thirty years, he became one of the most famous athletes in the world.

Pelé was a genius on the soccer field and a charming, outgoing person off the field. He could run 100 yards in under ten seconds. He had great timing and leaping ability, and was very creative in his play. "A good player will be thinking maybe two moves ahead," commented one national coach, "but Pelé can think six or seven moves ahead."

17

Mikael Hjuler of Denmark, like every player of his generation, was inspired by Pele.

Off the field, Pelé became an ambassador for soccer all over the world. His former coach once said, "When Pelé is in Spain, the people there think he is Spanish. When he is in England, they feel he is English. The same is true in other countries. Pelé is not an athlete; he is an international treasure."

Pelé's real name is Edson Arantes do Nascimento. He was born in the small rural town of Três Coraçoes. His father was an average soccer player who earned a modest living playing for a semiprofessional team. Pelé was convinced that his father was the greatest player in the world, and he longed to follow in his footsteps. He kept skipping school to play soccer, and soon the game became his whole life. When Pelé was eleven, a professional soccer player from the large Brazilian city of São Paulo spotted him playing and began coaching him. Four years later, Pelé had a tryout for a top professional squad in São Paulo but didn't make the team. So his coach took him to the coastal city of Santos, where he was hired by a junior team on a trial basis.

19

"I felt as if I was lost," Pelé said a few years later. "I was only fifteen, and suddenly I had to live with strange people in a strange, big place. I was scared of failing. . . ." Pelé's fears were soon relieved. Within a few months, he was promoted to one of the top teams in Santos, and by the time he was seventeen, he was playing for the Brazilian national team in the World Cup.

A former coach said of Pele: "He is an international treasure."

Argentina-2 Bulgaria-0

field, gathered his teammates around him for a quick pep talk. Whatever he said must have worked, because a few minutes later, Brazil scored twice to go ahead. Pelé then took over himself, tallying three goals in the second half to lead Brazil to a 5–2 win and a place in the finals against Sweden.

The Swedish coach predicted that the Brazilians would "panic all over the show" in the finals. But he didn't count on the calmness and determination of Brazil's young superstar. Pelé scored twice in the second half to break open a close game. One of his goals was a breathtaking juggling shot, in which he bounced the ball from foot to knee and back to his foot. The other goal was a spectacular header. Soccer had a new champion and a new king.

In the semifinal round in Sweden, Pelé proved that he was the team's leader. In a match against France, the Brazilians fell behind and slowly began to feel the game slipping away from them. Pelé, the youngest player on the

Before he retired from international competition, Pelé would lead Brazil to two more World Cup triumphs in 1962 and 1970. The South American team would thus become the first three-time winner of the tournament and the Jules Rimet Trophy.

Pele's determined genius led Brazil to three World Cup victories.

After the 1970 World Cup champion-ship, Pelé retired. He had scored an amazing 1,220 goals in 1,254 games during his career. No other soccer player has ever come close to that feat.

Scotland and Uruguay—and their different playing styles—clashed in this match.

STYLES COLLIDE

The speed and passing skills of Pelé and other Brazilian stars helped create a new offensive style for soccer that has been adopted by most Latin American teams and several top European squads. Meanwhile, many other European teams, notably the British and the Italians, have continued to play a more defensive brand of soccer. The Brazilian system calls for lots of short passes and quick moves toward the goal. Four players usually play up front on offense to attack the opponent's goal and three play back on defense. The British style calls for long passes and rough tackling, or sliding steals of the ball. Four players stay back on defense, and only three play up front on offense. Teams following the British style usually score fewer goals than those using the Brazilian style, but they generally give up fewer goals as well.

The Brazilian system also requires that a team have one or two great offensive stars, able to score just with individual effort. The British system calls for tougher players able to battle in the trenches.

NEW HEROES

The British style triumphed in 1966, and for the next four years many soccer teams around the world concentrated on defense. Then Brazil came back in 1970 with a great offensive display to overwhelm the Italian defense 4–1 in the Cup final. Pelé retired after that game, and his position as soccer's king was passed to some new heroes.

When Pele retired in 1970, he was still soccer's best player.

The first of these heroes were West Germany's Franz Beckenbauer and Holland's Johan Cruyff. Beckenbauer was a master of strategy, and Cruyff was one of the quickest men ever to play world-class soccer. Beckenbauer's quick thinking helped West Germany get past an exciting Polish team to reach the finals in the 1974 World Cup in Germany. The West Germany–Poland game was played on a muddy field covered with deep puddles of water. The Poles simply could not get their footing all day, and their running and long-passing game fell apart. Meanwhile, Beckenbauer figured out how to scoop the ball out of the puddles instead of making ground passes. The Germans controlled the action for much of the game and came away with a 1–0 victory. They were set to meet The Netherlands and its star Cruyff in the finals.

26

Like the '74 finals, every World Cup match is filled with thrilling plays.

A crowd of nearly 78,000 frenzied fans packed the stadium in Munich for the match. The fans were stunned when, only ninety seconds into the game, Cruyff broke into the open and was pulled down in the goal area. That meant a penalty kick for the Dutch. For a penalty kick, a single player goes one-on-one against the goalie. Holland's captain Johan Neeskens took the penalty shot and scored.

27

Franz Beckenbauer

The Germans scored on a penalty shot of their own less than thirty minutes later to tie the game. Then Cruyff made another rush as the Dutch fans in the stadium rose to their feet. He sent a beautiful pass to a teammate, who shot the ball quickly but directly into the German goalie's hands. The Dutch fans groaned; their heroes were unable to break through the Germans' iron defense. West Germany broke the tie just before halftime, and then "Kaiser" Beckenbauer and his mates turned back several more Dutch attacks in the second half to preserve a 2–1 win.

Four years later, the World Cup was played in South America again, with Argentina winning the tournament on its home turf. For the next several years, however, South American soccer seemed to decline. There were no Pelés or Vavas to lead the way. South American fans began looking desperately for a new hero. They found him in a small but powerful Argentine named Diego Armando Maradona. Even before the 1982 Cup in Spain, Maradona's excellent play had earned him the nickname "San Diego" (Saint Diego). With Maradona leading the way, Argentina was expected to challenge Italy for the 1982 title. However, Argentina's opponents concentrated on stopping Maradona, sometimes illegally. He was continually fouled during the early matches in Spain and was injured on several occasions. Without a healthy Maradona, the Argentines were unable to reach the finals.

Two European teams, the Italians and the West Germans, faced off for the 1982 Cup. The Italians had a wide-open offensive attack built around their high-scoring forward Paulo Rossi. As in 1974 against The Netherlands, the West Germans concentrated on defense. However, this time they weren't as successful, and Rossi's two goals powered Italy to a 3–1 win.

Italy battled to the 1982 finals behind the play of Paulo Rossi (at right).

South American fans were counting on Maradona to put that continent back on top in the soccer world four years later. San Diego was healthy and in top form in 1986 in Mexico. He earned a new nickname during that championship, "El Rey" (the King). Before a semifinal match between Argentina and Belgium, the Belgian goalie made the foolish comment "Maradona is nothing special." He soon regretted those words, as San Diego chipped in a left-footed shot early in the second half for a 1–0 Argentine lead and then made a solo rush for the game's only other score.

Argentina's Jorge Burruchaga scored the winning goal in the finals.

Maradona was closely shadowed and pushed around throughout the final match against West Germany. Nevertheless, he helped set up the two Argentine goals in a game that was tied 2–2 with just six minutes remaining. Then Maradona picked up a loose ball and sent a rifle pass through four West German defenders to teammate Jorge Burruchaga, who was on a dead run heading toward the German goal. No one else in the world could have made that pass. Burruchaga didn't have to break stride as he converted the pass into the winning score. As the ball went into the net, a roar went up in Mexico City that could probably be heard in Buenos Aires, Argentina's capital city. Posters were soon flying on streets throughout Buenos Aires declaring, "MARADONA PRESIDENTE!" Soccer had a new king, and the world had a new hero.

Like Argentina's World Cup victory in 1986, the 1970 World Cup final between Brazil and Italy had provided many memorable moments. Now, as the game entered the second half, the score was tied 1–1.

Diego Maradona emerged as Argentina's hero during the 1986 World Cup.

Play began just as it had ended in the first half—up and down the field the players raced, closely shadowing each other's moves. But this was to be Brazil's day in the end. With Pelé leading the way with daring rushes and passes, the Brazilians scored three straight goals in the second half and left the field carrying the Jules Rimet Trophy. As the first team in soccer history to win the World Cup championship three times, the Brazilians were allowed to keep one of the world's most-famous trophies for good. A new cup would have to be made for the next World Cup tournament four years later.

Pelé was the star of the 1970 World Cup final; Diego Maradona was the soccer hero of the 1980s. Who will succeed them in the 1990s? That hero might come for the first time from the United States or the Soviet Union. Neither country has been a World Cup power in the past, but both are on the rise now.

Old rivalries will also continue in the 1990s, as European and Latin American powers battle in World Cup tournaments to determine where the best soccer is played. Fans in these countries will continue to be fanatics, cheering wildly for their heroes and imitating them in school yards and open fields everywhere.

The World Cup will remain a unique mixture of athletic excellence and high emotional drama in the 1990s and beyond. It is the championship of the world's favorite sport, and it provides great moments unlike any other event in sports.

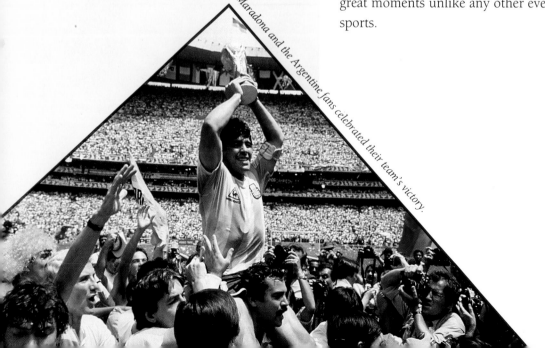

Maradona and the Argentine fans celebrated their team's victory.